Stretching

Educise
4 Kids
EDUCATION & EXERCISE FOR KIDS

Created By
Priscilla Fauvette

Illustrated By
Bernard Fauvette

Anatomy

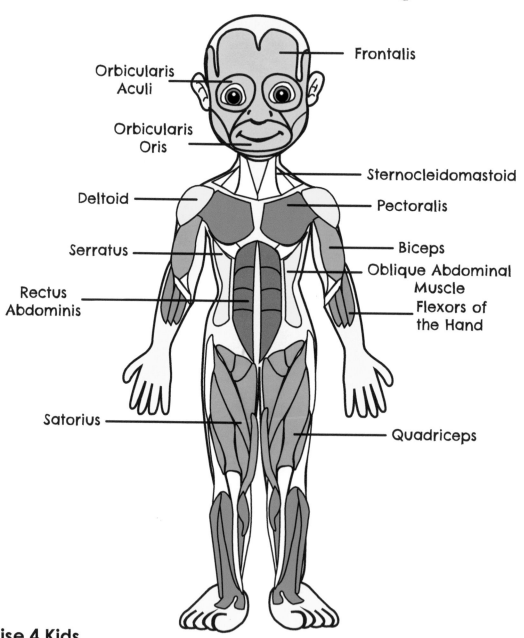

Frontalis

Orbicularis Aculi

Orbicularis Oris

Sternocleidomastoid

Deltoid

Pectoralis

Serratus

Biceps

Oblique Abdominal Muscle

Rectus Abdominis

Flexors of the Hand

Satorius

Quadriceps

Anatomy

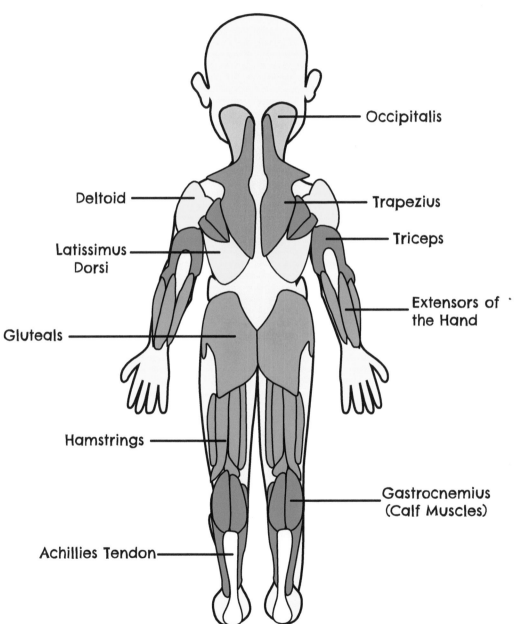

Occipitalis

Deltoid

Trapezius

Triceps

Latissimus
Dorsi

Extensors of
the Hand

Gluteals

Hamstrings

Gastrocnemius
(Calf Muscles)

Achillies Tendon

Glute & Hamstring Stretch

Sit on the floor

Stretch out your legs

Bend one knee over your other leg

Gentle pull that knee to the left

Hold this for 5 seconds

Let's do this to the other side

Neck Stretch

Stand up straight

Put your feet apart

Place one hand on the side of your head

Gently pull your head to the left

Hold this for 5 seconds

Let's do this to the other side

Shoulder Stretch

Stand up straight

Put your feet together

Bring one arm across your body

Gentle press on your elbow

Press your arm towards your body

Hold this for 5 seconds

Let's do this to the other side

Quadricep Stretch

Stand up straight

Bend one leg up behind your body

Hold this with your arm

Bring one arm out for balance

Hold this for 5 seconds

Let's do this to the other side

Hip Flexor & Glute Stretch

Stand up straight

Kneel one knee on the floor

Place one hand on your knee

Slowly lean forward

Hold this for 5 seconds

Let's do this to the other side

Chest & Shoulder Stretch

Stand up straight

Put your feet together

Place your hands behind your back

Lock your hands together

Stretch them gently backwards

Hold this for 5 seconds

Abdominal Stretch

Lay face down on the floor

Place your hands underneath

Push your body up gently

Bend your back and look forward

Hold this for 5 seconds

Tricep Stretch

Stand up straight
Put your feet together
Stretch both your arms up
Bend one arm place it on your back
Place your other hand on your elbow
Pull your elbow gently back
Hold this for 5 seconds
Let's do this to the other side

Inner Leg Stretch

Sit on the floor

Bring the soles of your feet together

Hold your feet with your hands

Place your elbows on your knees

Gently press your knees down with your elbows

Hold this for 5 seconds

Back Stretch

Kneel on the floor

Stretch your arms forward

Slowly lower yourself to the floor

Hold this for 5 seconds

Whole Body Stretch

Lay on your back on the floor

Stretch your arms out

Stretch your legs out

Hold this for 5 seconds

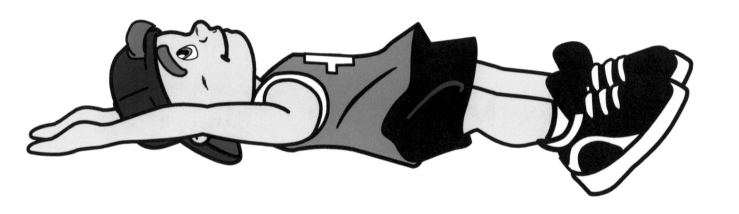

Calf Stretch

Stand up straight near a wall
Place one foot in front
Slightly bend your front knee
Stretch out your back leg
Hold this for 5 seconds
Let's do this to the other side

Hamstring & Calf Stretch

Sit on the floor

Stretch out one leg

Bend your other knee

Place your foot on your thigh

Reach out and touch your toes

Hold this for 5 seconds

Let's do this to the other side

Bicep Stretch

Stand up straight
Put your feet together
Bring one arm in front of your body
Turn your palm and face it up
Gently pull your hand backwards
Hold this for 5 seconds
Let's do this to the other side

Hamstring & Glutes Stretch

Lay on your back on the floor

Bring one knee to your chest

Place your hands on your knee

Gently press your knee towards your body

Hold this for 5 seconds

Let's do this to the other side

Keep an eye out for the rest of the series

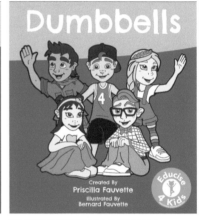

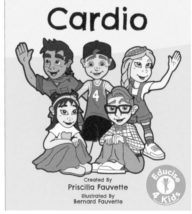

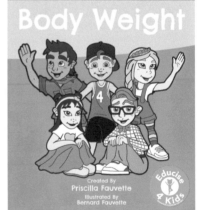

CPSIA information can be obtained
at www.ICGtesting.com
Printed in the USA
LVHW071425250322
714381LV00002B/58

9 780648 534747